All Scriptures are from the Olive Tree Bible King James Version

Cover Design: J. Alison
Back Cover Photo: Mike Preston Photography: 145 S Lincolnway | North Aurora, Il 60542
Interior Design: Janie Lee
Published by: 220 Publishing

We Dream: Understanding God's Voice in the Night. J. Alison. First Edition.
ISBN: 978-1-5136-6412-5

TABLE OF CONTENTS

I dedicate this book to my 2 daughters, Rochelle and Niya, and my two grandsons, Emir and Shaun, who are the inspiration for every goal I have.

To my dear daughter/friend Cametha Games who, like the marathon runner that she is, put her hand in my back and pushed me up the last hill until I reached the top and could see the finish line.

To Silk Faith Walker and Glenn Murray who were literally the inspiration sent by God to encourage me to begin writing.

And to all of you who never let me rest and challenged me to write...I thank you.

Dreams have always been a means of solidifying the communications of the Sovereign One to humanity. During our sleep our minds are more susceptible to receiving the communications of God easier. The normal course of a day, for many, is filled with never-ending assignments and distractions. This is one reason why The Lord deals with us in the night.

Job 33:15-19 details how, during the night, *God will open our ears and seal* His instructions. Therefore, accurately interpreting our dreams is essential to keeping our connection with God fortified. This dimension of gifting is rare and void of readily available instructors armed with revelation and principles to help Believers in this realm.

Prophet J. Alison is a skillful craftsman in the realm of the prophetic, with an unusual grace for dream interpretation. Our ministry, Rivers Chicago, and those joined to us have benefited tremendously from her mantle. I'm certain you will be blessed immensely as you follow the pattern clearly laid out in this blueprint for dream interpretation.

I affirm *We Dream: Understanding God's Voice in The Night* and put my blessing on it. May it serve as a major nexus in helping you and those you are called to serve fulfill eternity's commission. Pay attention to your dreams for the Most High is speaking.

Apostle Stephen A. Garner
Rivers of Living Water Ministries Int'l
Chicago, IL USA

CHAPTER ONE: FIRST THINGS FIRST

How old were you when you had your first dream? Or a better question; How old were you when you started remembering your dreams? Did you journal them? Did you chalk them up as something you ate, or did you just forget about them because you had no one to interpret their meanings?

Well, let's start this conversation by saying this: Dreams are the gateway to our future. One of the roadmaps to our life. God instructs, counsels, and warns through dreams. War strategies were given in dreams, and nations were brought to rubble because of a dream. God revealed an enemy's ambush strategy to His chosen ones through the prophetic *(II Kings 6:12)* as well as how to prepare for the future by way of a dream *(Gen 41:25-36)*.

Although every dream is not from God, He uses them to stop man from destroying their future *(Job 33:14-16)*. He reveals the error in the plan of the dreamer and releases a better plan that will bring success. Some ignore their dreams, consider them trash and not to be taken seriously. I recently read a commentary by an author that insisted dreams are not prophetic, but rather are quite useless. I assure you that statement couldn't be further from the truth. Your dreams are very important. They are God's voice in the night, full of instruction and if heeded will usher you into triumph.

As you read this book, it is my goal to take you into the mind of a dream interpreter and help you to accurately dissect the meaning of your dreams.

LITERAL VS SYMBOLIC

One of the most common mistakes made by the dreamer is to assume the dream is literal. If one dreams about a friend, the automatic assumption is to apply the meaning of the dream to the life of the friend when in actuality, the friend represents some aspect of the dreamer or someone in real life who is similar to the person in the dream. Unless you have the gift of interpretation, which is commonplace among prophets and prophetic people, most dreams are messages to the dreamer.

Literal versus symbolic carries a basic rule. If everything in the dream can be tied back to the actual object and people in current life, then the dream has a literal message. But if one thing turns out to be a symbolic representation then the entire dream is symbolic and no longer literal. For example, if you drive to the job location you currently work at, talk to the boss you currently work for and go to the cafeteria at your job where you routinely eat, the entire dream can be based on a literal interpretation. A literal message. But if you drive to the theater you were in the night before, walk up to a cashier's window to pay for your theater ticket just like you did the night before, but the cashier is a full-grown talking bear, the entire dream has now become symbolic rather than literal because the bear is a symbol of something since we all know bears can't talk or work as a cashier in a theater.

For God speaketh once, Yea twice, though man regardeth it not. In a dream, in a vision of the night, When deep sleep falleth upon men, In slumberings upon the bed; Then he openeth the ears of men, And sealeth their instruction, That he may withdraw man from his purpose, And hide pride from man; He keepeth back his soul from the pit, And his life from perishing by the sword (Job 33:14-18).

When you read that passage it clearly is a message to the dreamer instructing him to change something in his/her life in order to avoid an unfavorable outcome. It says the objective of the dream is to withdraw man from his own purpose and protect him from the spirit of pride. So therefore, when interpreting your dream, you should automatically assume it is about you.

Oftentimes, God will send urgent warnings through dreams. The following example is one that I vividly recall.

A bride-to-be sent me a dream she had a few months before her wedding was to take place. Her fiancé had the "exact" same "type" of dream a couple of days apart from hers. She reasoned that both were suffering from wedding anxiety, which resulted in the dreams.

Her dream began at the opening of the wedding ceremony. She was in her dressing room, along with the Maid of Honor, and couldn't find her wedding dress. She ended up wearing a black dress that she just so happened to bring along with other incidentals. She was so upset that she couldn't find her wedding dress, but she was determined that the wedding would go on. The traditional wedding song, "Here Comes the Bride", began to play. She emerged from her dressing room and walked to the opening of the church sanctuary, ready to walk down the aisle. As she was walking and looking up at the sunshine coming through a window to the left side of the sanctuary, she noticed she had her dress on backwards. When she met her husband-to-be at the altar, he grabbed her hand, and they turned to face the minister. As the minister began to speak, to their surprise the language sounded like witchcraft. She said she became upset and didn't understand what was going on and the dream ended.

Her fiancé's dream was just as strange. While in his dressing room preparing to get ready, he realized he forgot his tux and brought a t-shirt and pants with him instead. He sent his brother to run out and pick up a tux right quick, but instead of returning with a tuxedo, he came back with a jean outfit. By this time, he has no other choice but to wear the jeans and jacket. He felt his brother made the wrong purchase on purpose because earlier, he caught him flirting with his fiancé.

As he goes to stand at the altar and wait for his Bride, he decided to peek in on her as he passed by her dressing room. She was upset when she saw him because that action has long been viewed as "bad luck" on the day of the wedding. As he stands with his brother (the Best Man) at the altar, the traditional song, "Here Comes the Bride", begins to play, and the dream ended.

When this dream was sent to me, it made me sad for them because after reading it, I instantly knew they were not to get married. A dress on backwards clearly indicated she was headed in the wrong direction by marrying him. The dress being black means she had no substance within her to be a wife at this time in her life. The sun shining from the left side of the church was significant because "left" represents weakness, which was why the left side of the church stood out to her in the dream. It represents the extreme weakness of this soon to be union. Her fiancé's outfit being a jean outfit revealed their complete incompatibility for each other. Neither one had on the proper mantle for marriage. Upset with his brother's flirting was really a depiction of himself. His inability to trust. Glancing in on the Bride before the wedding showed certain doom. Both of them hearing the traditional wedding song was the only thing in their dreams that matched. The reason for this was that the song reveals their strong desire to be married. I sent her the interpretation, and she was furious with me. She stopped speaking and blocked me from all access to her.

A word to you who can interpret: Never hold back the truth for fear of consequences. It's better to warn someone of upcoming destruction rather than to have spiritual blood on your hands.

CHAPTER TWO: GIFTING OR THEORY?

God is speaking to you about your life in your dream. If He cannot get your attention due to the hustle and bustle of your life, He waits until you are asleep, and then deposits a message into your soul. The dream's purpose is to put you on the right path.

God gives us dreams because He wants to interject Himself into our life plans, change our thinking, get us turned around in the right direction. He gives us dreams to position us for something that is coming, to correct us, or to reveal to us something that has been hidden.

So, how do you begin to learn dream interpretation? You start out by recording your dream as soon as you wake up. Write it down or record it into a voice memo. If you don't have time to record the entire dream, at least jot down or record a couple of things that will jog your memory, so you won't forget the entire dream. The core message is usually within the first scene of the dream. Sometimes it is repeated throughout the dream in different scenes.

If you didn't have a chance to properly record the dream, once you get a chance, go back to your notes or recording and finish documenting the dream in its entirety, describing every detail of the dream. If your dream is full of symbols (e.g., white horse, leaking roof, red shoes), make a separate list writing down what each one of the symbols mean. (Refer to glossary) Once you have made your list, replace the symbol in the dream with the word that interprets the symbol. Go back and re-read the dream with the symbol interpretations in place. This is step one in interpreting.

Almost every object and person in the dream will have its own interpretation. People, colors, animals, vehicles, numbers and rooms all stand for something.

Once again, remember for the most part, people will represent some aspect of the dreamer's personality, personal habits or that of someone else the dreamer knows. If you are a prophet or prophetic person who interprets dreams regularly, this rule may not apply.

BASIC RULES

I cannot emphasize this rule enough. Unless you have the gift to interpret, and God begins to show you the secrets of men's hearts for counsel, almost every dream the dreamer has is a message to the dreamer. Once again, even if recognizable faces are in the dream, the dream is a message to the one who dreamt it.

Every dream begins with a location. The location in the dream holds a clue. Here are some examples. If your dream begins in a living room, typically it is about something that is currently happening. Something is being revealed. The basement indicates hidden things or things possibly of a base nature. The people present in the location are just as important as the location itself. As you refer to the glossary, you will be able to begin to put your dream together like pieces of a puzzle. Once you identify the core theme, you can continue to unravel and piece together each scene until the entire message unfolds.

COLORS

Colors are important interpretation markers.A woman having a dream wearing a pair of red high heel shoes reveals something about her character. Wearing a brown coat represents dead works. The color brown is void of life and the coat is one's covering, occupation or profession. It can also represent a gifting or mantle. Another basic rule: Colors rarely have "dual" meanings unlike other objects or representations. Animals can have dual meanings based on their God-given nature and creative purpose. People in dreams can take on several different meanings depending on the storyline of the dream, but colors are typically static in definition. So, if the color is red, it's going to fall along the lines of passion, anger, hot. If the color is pink, it's going to typically represent lust, carnality, or something fleshly in nature. (Refer to the glossary)

BUILDINGS, STRUCTURE AND PLACES

If the dream took place in a house, record which room in the house the dream took place. Also, if possible, record whose house it was (e.g., grandmother's, childhood home, friend's house, boss's home, etc.). Whatever type of structure the dream took place in, record details about the space. If it took place in an airport and the airport was "empty", that is an important clue. An airport represents a large ministry, work or even traveling to a destination literally or figuratively. Arriving to an empty airport reveals an error is happening or about to happen in the dreamer's life. It is a warning. If your dream begins in the bedroom, God is dealing with secret things. Intimate things. Sometimes God reveals instructions to you on how to deal with something only you know about. The Word says in Psalm 4:4, *Stand in awe, and sin not:*

commune with your own heart upon your bed, and be still. Another interesting room for a dream setting is the kitchen. The kitchen is a place we create things. The kitchen deals with matters of the heart. Matthew 12:35 says, *A good man out of the good treasure of the heart bringeth forth good things; and an evil man out of the evil treasure bringeth forth evil things.* Another place that "reveals" is the roof. However, please note that a roof can have other meanings. In Acts 11:5-12, the Apostle Peter described a trance. It took place on a rooftop and contained a life-changing message for the church. Up until that point, the Jews would not preach the Gospel of Jesus Christ or Baptism of the Holy Ghost to the Gentiles. The Jews felt they were high in stature and wouldn't culturally mix with them. The Jews also had a custom of not eating certain animals that were considered to be unclean. God lowered a sheet on the roof full of unclean animals and told Peter to kill the animals and eat them, but he refused. The scene repeated three times, and all three times Peter would not eat the animals. After the 3rd time, the Lord told Peter, "What God has made clean do not call unclean." At that very moment, 3 men were knocking at the door of the house. They told Peter they were instructed to take him to a man's house that was waiting to hear the gospel. When they arrived, the man was a Gentile.

God showed Peter in the dream how the message of salvation was not for the Jews only, but for the whole world. It was "revealed" on a rooftop.

The setting of the dream can be anywhere: a movie theater, a concert hall, etc. The message in the dream is wrapped up in practically every aspect of the dream, which includes the place or the building where the dream takes place.

ANIMALS IN DREAMS

An animal in the scene of the dream will be very important in the interpretation of the scene simply due to the nature of the animal. A snake in a dream will be centered around deception, being caught unaware. An ant in the dream concerns building something. Termites represent the destruction of some-thing. A turtle could represent slow progress in a situation. Note the natural God-given nature of the animal in the dream and apply it to the message.

NUMBERS

Numbers are descriptions. They are definitions. Numbers can identify times and seasons. If you were 12 years of age in a dream, the indication could be something from your past. Numbers are dream an-chors. Why anchors? Because they connect securely to the meaning of the dream. They are significant clues to the interpretation. For instance, the number 15 means free, liberty and honor. So, say you had a dream and voting was in the dream in addition to the number 15; there would be a weighty significance attached to the interpretation of that particular number because the 15th Amendment of the Con-stitution states, "The right of citizens of the United States to vote shall not be denied or abridged by the United States or by any State on account of race, color, or previous condition of servitude." That amendment speaks of freedom and liberty which is what the number 15 means. So, it is important to pay attention to all numbers that stand out in your dreams.

GOVERNMENT

Dream interpretations are very necessary in the governmental level of prophecy. Prophets have to be able to do more than just release "a word". They have to be able to release strategies, edicts, consequences and judgments. Oftentimes those directives come through dreams.

It is important to be able to strategize according to a released dream for an upcoming event, an upcoming challenge or even an unforeseen attack. God releases the plans and strategies of victory for a people. For a nation.

In Daniel chapter 2, God gave King Nebuchadnezzar a dream that spoke into the future concerning five different kingdoms. God will give you explicit instructions regarding upcoming seasons in a dream.

We must understand them.

So, to answer the question, Is dream interpretation gifting or theory? It's oftentimes a combination of both.

CHAPTER THREE: PEOPLE

One of the most common mistakes the dreamer makes when interpreting a dream is face recognition. Friends and relatives, dead or alive, are commonplace characters in our dreams. The dreamer's friend, relative or even coworker will carry a message about the dreamer. God will even use a person with the same initials and personality to reveal a message that may apply to a completely different person, and this person will be someone the dreamer knows. The exception to this rule: If you are a person with the gift to interpret, anything goes and you will experience many interpretations that are about the person "in" the dream rather than the dreamer.

Deceased loved ones will often show up in our

dreams immediately after laying them to rest. We must understand that this is not our loved one. It is a familiar spirit. The door to that spirit needs to be closed immediately in order to put a halt to any attempts to contaminate our dreams. If you're thinking, "I didn't open any door, so why do I need to close one?" Relatives are a part of our generational bloodline, and as a result, a familiar spirit can have immediate access after the relative transitions. If necessary, you must be diligent in denying access to the spirit. People who have passed cannot come back to earth and give us messages to follow. Those are familiar spirits sent by the adversary to deposit messages into our dream state that are not connected to our purpose or destiny. The following biblical passage speaks to this:

Luke 16:24-31, *And he cried and said, Father Abraham, have mercy on me, and send Lazarus, that he may dip the tip of his finger in water, and cool my tongue; for I am tormented in this flame. But Abraham said, Son, remember that thou in thy lifetime receivedst thy good things, and likewise Lazarus evil things: but now he is comforted, and thou art tormented. And beside all this, between us and you there is a great gulf fixed: so that they which would pass from hence to you cannot; neither can they pass to us, that would come from thence. Then he said, I pray thee therefore, father, that thou wouldest send him to my father's house: For I have five brethren; that he may testify unto them, lest they also come into this place of torment. Abraham saith unto him, They have Moses and the prophets; let them hear them. And he said, Nay, father Abraham: but if one went unto them from the dead, they will repent. And he said unto him, If they hear not Moses and the prophets, neither will they be persuaded, though one rose from the dead.*

In addition, if you experience dreams that showcase a familiar deceased person giving you explicit instructions, the Word says to "try the spirit". I John 4:1, *Beloved, believe not every spirit, but try the spirits whether they are of God: because many false prophets are gone out into the world.*

I once had a dear friend who unexpectedly died in his sleep at a young age. This individual was a minister of music, widely known and extremely popular. People were devastated upon hearing of his death. I began to post pictures of him on my social media platform and speak of him often. Soon afterward, a familiar spirit imitating his presence began to show up in my dreams. After the 3rd appearance, I realized what was happening, and I immediately shut down that spirit's access in prayer. Upon doing that, the dreams instantly stopped.

You are the strongman of your house and therefore must use your authority to guard your access gate. As previously mentioned, living people who show up in your dream are an intricate part of the dream's puzzle. They could represent a single characteristic of the dreamer or even possess the same type of habit the Lord wants to break. Your mother and your grandmother showing up in your dreams rarely, if at all, are a representation of themselves. The same rule applies to sisters and brothers. You have to analyze the person's character, personality or both and determine what about them is part of the dream's message? Once you do that, insert that piece of interpretation into the place they hold in the dream.

WORLD PERSONALITIES IN DREAMS

Whenever God places an extremely recognizable and popular personality in your dream (e.g., a politician, an entertainer, a well-known actor, a famous athlete), more often than not, they represent an aspect of something or someone within the dream. God will place famous personalities in your dream in order to "showcase" the specific message. The basic rule regarding a world personality in your dream: That personality has been placed in your dream as a "defining marker". They could represent any one of the following: virtue, evil, pride, arrogance, benevolence, charity, administration, governmental authority, a person the dreamer knows or doesn't know, etc. No matter what the personality represents, it will be a significant clue to unraveling the meaning of the dream.

CHAPTER FOUR:
PATTERNS AND REPETITIONS

Each year you dream, it's a snapshot into your life. Whatever God is speaking to you about during the year is reflected in the catalog of your dreams. That is why it is important to organize your dream journal chronologically.

When you begin to pay attention and journal your dreams, you may notice certain dream patterns. Dream patterns may become repetitious depending on what season you're in. For example, if you are in a season of elevation, you will begin to notice every dream has an underlying message of correction and sometimes warnings. Why? Because prior to elevation, God will begin a new discipline within you, requiring the elimination of unproductive habits.

Here is an example of a dream pattern. There was

a woman in ministry who was experiencing a season of elevation. God was releasing a greater level of authority, but it required her to work on her heart. In order to get this message to her, God started showing her dreams about a suitcase. A suitcase represents your "heart" (Refer to glossary). In her first dream, her and her younger daughter were going on a trip to visit a couple of her girlfriends. When they arrived at the house, to her surprise, there were several women at the house that she had never met. She was irritated by the additional women, and her daughter tried to reason with her suggesting it would be fun to meet new people; but she had no desire to meet, much less spend time with, new people. She only wanted to be with her friends. In addition, she didn't even realize she had forgotten to pack and bring a suitcase until she arrived at the house.

Several months later the Lord gave her another dream about a suitcase. In this dream, she arrived at an airport with her oldest daughter to catch a flight taking her to another state where she would be participating in ministry. She had no idea her mother had already boarded the plane. When she arrived and boarded, it was a plane full of suites similar to hotel suites. Each passenger and their accompanying parties had their own suite. Her suite was smaller than the suite next door, but it was still very nice. When she looked down at her suitcase, she suddenly remembered, she forgot to pack. In her suitcase was a couple of old articles of clothing but nothing suitable to wear to the conference. Her mother didn't even bring a suitcase. She said to her mother, "I forgot to pack! I don't have anything to wear!" Her mother replied, "Neither do I, but I'll just buy new clothes when I get there." Her daughter was the only one who had packed a full suitcase the night before. One last thing to note, her suite had two twin beds. The suite next door had 2 queen-size beds.

The interpretation: God showed the dreamer three generations of the heart. The airplane suites represented elevation in ministry with a new level of authority. The twin beds versus queen beds represent the promotion at its first level. The mother of the dreamer and daughter of the dreamer were only symbols and not a real part of the ministry trip. The mother without a suitcase was a message to the dreamer about where she inherited her ability to have a "cold-heart". Her mother had no suitcase at all, which means the person struggles with having a heart of compassion. The daughter of the dreamer having a full suitcase indicates a "loving heart"; and God was showing the dreamer that this has to be the goal. The dreamer having a suitcase with a couple of items in it reveals some progress concerning the heart compared to the previous dream where she showed up with no suitcase at all. However, with this promotion, she must work on having a "loving heart". She cannot exclude people as she did in her first dream. She must work on sincerely being compassionate and loving to people.

God will also sound an alarm through dream patterns. Sometimes God will show you a great loss to come as a warning to change course, and the more you ignore, the more the dream will repeat. Dream patterns can also be a foretelling of a season. If the season is going to be a hard one, a repeat pattern of this type of dream is set in motion. For example, you may notice every dream you "now" have is set in winter. The scenes of each dream will vary, but it's always in winter. These are foretelling dreams of a challenging time to come. God often gives relatives repeating dreams of an impending death of another relative in order to prepare the dreamer for the transition. Spouses have reported seeing their partner's death months or years before it happened, and despite the repeated dreams, it was still difficult to be ready. I'll give you an example. I have a relative whose husband abruptly died. It was heart breaking because he seemingly had no serious health issues that could explain a sudden death. For an entire year prior to his passing, the Lord kept giving her dreams of losing her purse. The scenario in each dream was different, but the central message was the loss of her purse. Now a purse can represent several things including your personality, character, or temperament; but in this case, it represented Matthew 6:21, *For where your treasure is, there will your heart be also.* Her husband was her treasure, and in each dream, she lost her purse and could never find it. The purse represented her husband, and the Lord was revealing to her she was about to lose him.

If you have a dream that is a clear warning, it requires immediate action. Here are some examples:

1. Having your car repeatedly stolen in dreams is a warning and requires immediate action.
2. Someone familiar to you in real life always showing up as a villain in repeated dreams requires immediate action.
3. Having repeated dreams where you arrive late for an important event requires immediate action.

Dreams with warnings are requiring you to change course and correct a behavior. The following are dream patterns that may require an intervention of intercessory deliverance prayer:

- **Always being chased in a dream**
- **Jolted out of a nightmare**
- **Always falling**
- **Often being murdered**
- **Participating in dream sex**
- **Looking forward to dream sex**
- **Being physically pinned down in dreams**
- **Your molester shows up in your dreams**
- **Being raped in dreams**
- **Being stabbed in dreams**

If you can answer yes to experiencing one of these dream patterns, it's highly likely you are a candidate for deliverance, or at the very least, there's a need to command the entity that is invading your sleep state to leave in Jesus' name. God does not want you to be afraid of dreaming. Proverbs 3:24 says, *When thou liest down, thou shalt not be afraid: yea, thou shalt lie down, and thy sleep shall be sweet.*

I have interviewed several people, and after a brief conversation, it was obvious they've been continually tormented or warned while dreaming.

The following passages of scriptures are examples of God warning through dreams.

Matthew 2:7-14, *Then Herod, when he had privily called the wise men, enquired of them diligently what time the star appeared. And he sent them to Bethlehem, and said, Go and search diligently for the young child; and when ye have found him, bring me word again, that I may come and worship him also. When they had heard the king, they departed; and, lo, the star, which they saw in the east, went before them, till it came and stood over where the young child was. When they saw the star, they rejoiced with exceeding great joy.*

And when they were come into the house, they saw the young child with Mary his mother, and fell down, and worshipped him: and when they had opened their treasures, they presented unto him gifts; gold, and frankincense, and myrrh. And being warned of God in a dream that they should not return to Herod, they departed into their own country another way. And when they were departed, behold, the angel of the Lord appeareth to Joseph in a dream, saying, Arise, and take the young child and his mother, and flee into Egypt, and be thou there until I bring thee word: for Herod will seek the young child to destroy him. When he arose, he took the young child and his mother by night and departed into Egypt.

Repetitious dreams are a sign of one of two things: One, you are not paying attention to the message God is sending or two, there is something coming "very soon" and you are not prepared. Repetitions are God's grace, patience and favor. Chances are you have had the dream more than twice, now making it an urgent message. Repetitious dreams typically hold messages of decision and directives. These dreams, if ignored, can be consequential. Common symbols in these types of dreams are vehicles, shoes, purses, wallets, familiar houses, familiar people, and minimal variation in the story line. Typically, there is a deadline attached to understanding the message, thus the reason for the repetition.

For whatever reason, God seems to make dreams of repetition some of the most difficult dreams to interpret for the dreamer. One can assume the reason for this is that God is bringing frustration upon the dreamer which is a reflection of His frustration with the dreamer's apathy. Just when you settle down, stop feeling anxious and forget about the troubling dream, it resurfaces.

I once had a repeating dream for five years. In each dream, my car was stolen. Every single time I would have the dream, I would wake up troubled and eventually fearful about what the interpretation could be. The dreams would be very short, but the end was always the same. One time I went to visit a friend, came out of the house to leave and my car was gone. Another time I went into a building for what seemed like a visit to a warehouse, came out to leave and my car was gone. Another dream setting was a gas station. I went there with my daughter, who in real life was fully grown with a young baby but in the dream, she was an adolescent, which indicated a timeline of negligence. I left the car running, and when I returned it was in the process of being driven away.

I had tons of the same type of dream until I couldn't rest about them any longer. The automobile represented the gift of prophecy which I had all but completely stopped using and as a result, God was warning me that I was not going to be able to operate in ministry because I wouldn't have the power due to neglecting the gift. So needless to say, I stopped procrastinating, and immediately the dreams stopped. When you come into compliance with what God wants you to do, your chastising dreams will come to a screeching halt.

If your destiny is in a holding pattern due to your neglect, you will begin to have repetitious dreams with the intent to invoke you to act. Each one may have a different storyline, but the core message will be the same. Here is a similar example using a car with a slightly different twist. You dreamt a friend totaled your car. Next you dreamt you left your car parked illegally, and it was towed. Next you dreamt you double-parked your car while running into a store, and when you returned, the car had been side swiped. In the final dream, you went to visit a friend and parked your car five blocks away. After the visit, you walk to your car and discover the back window is broken and an expensive book left on the back-seat was taken. The central object in all four dreams is the car. In all four dreams, the dreamer suffered a loss. The core message to the dreamer is that he/she is placing greater value on something other than what God is calling the dreamer to do. The dreamer has been careless and apathetic about his/her life's purpose (represented by the automobile), thereby creating entry for the adversary to steal and destroy.

CHAPTER FIVE: INTERPRETING THE DREAMS OF OTHERS

Interpreting the dream of others is a combination of gift, theory and supernatural revelation. If you have the gift to interpret, most people will prefer to tell you the dream in a conversation rather than to write it down and send it to you. You may experience a person deciding to forego interpretation because they considered it too much of an inconvenience to transcribe their dream. The reason why writing a dream down is important is because you remember much more when you begin to write. You will recall details in the dream that you otherwise would not remember by only having a conversation about the dream. If a person insists on telling the dream rather than writing it down, request a recording attached to an email.

Once you receive the dream it may be necessary for you to send the dreamer additional questions in order to get all the facts about the dream. Details, current events, and background information are examples of important pieces to the puzzle when attempting to interpret.

You need to be able to identify the season of the dream. Is it a message from the dreamer's past, present or future? This is often determined by the location of the dream. As previously mentioned, if a scene is taking place in the living room, that's an indicator of current events. If the scene is taking place at the dreamer's childhood home, that is typically a message regarding some aspect of the dreamer's past (Refer to glossary).

You should always know what is "currently" going on in a person's life because that information is vital to the interpretation. It sometimes makes the difference between accuracy and inaccuracy—who the dream applies to and who it doesn't. Do not allow the person to treat you like a psychic, giving you skeletal information hoping you will unroll the scroll (so to speak) and read them their life story.

If you are a prophet or a prophetic person who has the gift to interpret, your gift has a mantle of purpose and it is important for you to identify it. God has not given you a gift to interpret dreams for popularity. The gift's purpose is to distinctly serve man in a pointed capacity, so that in the end it will bring glory to God.

Let's look at Joseph and Daniel. Both stood before kings who had disturbing dreams. Joseph stood before Pharaoh (Genesis 41) and Daniel stood before Nebuchadnezzar (Daniel 2). Both men were promoted politically because of their superior ability to interpret (Genesis 41:39-46; Daniel 2:48).

Joseph's purpose late in life was to provide for his lineage during the seven-year drought. God sent revelation through dream interpretation, clearly indicating Israel would need His supernatural provision during the drought.

Daniel and Joseph had several parallels throughout their lives. For instance, both were taken into exile, both were dream interpreters, both served kings and as a result were highly promoted. In addition, they both suffered great injustices. Unlike Daniel, Joseph was soul-tied to the Gentiles through marriage. He married a Gentile after his promotion.

Although there are several similarities, the one distinct difference was that Daniel's primary role was that of an intercessor (Daniel 6:10-11). He was an intercessor prior to his capture and exile. Throughout his life, he was continually placed in dreadful circumstances which called for supernatural deliverance. Daniel was an elderly man when faced with death in the lion's den. His promotional power and intercession were the forces that delivered his people.

MISINTERPRETING A DREAM

A warning to singles in relationships. Oftentimes, when you are in a relationship and you strongly desire to marry your partner, but they are resistant to marriage, it is not uncommon for the person who is "ready to marry" to begin to have dreams about marriage. The reason for this is there is usually a strong desire for marriage in the dreamer's prophetic stream, so the dreamer will begin to have dreams that appear to indicate future matrimony. The dreamer must look again at the dream and find the real message. Quite often there are messages within the dream that completely contradict the dreamer's real-life desire. Here is a personal story which is a typical example of this error in interpretation.

I was dating a man for several years and was convinced he was my husband. I had received prophecies confirming such; however, he did not want to get married. Although this made me question the validity of the prophecies, I refused to believe the relationship would not end in matrimony. In our third dating year, I began to have dreams that clearly pointed towards matrimony. In my head, I was making secret plans to marry, even daydreaming about our multiple car ownership and properties.

One night I had a dream I was in my boyfriend's home but wasn't supposed to be there. I was sneaking around the house. The strange thing about the dream was that it took place in his kitchen. The dream was in grayscale, but one item was in color and stood out in the dream. A small lapel pin fashioned after the American flag was lying on his kitchen counter. No matter how much I meditated on that symbol and its meaning, I could not interpret it.

Years later, long after the relationship ended, the interpretation became obvious. Why? Because my emotions were no longer involved. Kitchen represents the heart and the American flag represents "freedom/independence". The Lord was telling me that my significant other desired his independence more than matrimony and it was truly his "heart's desire".

Had I really paid attention to my dreams, it would have saved me frustration and sadness. But when your desire outweighs the truth, you will let your emotions be your guide. *The carnal mind is ruled by the lust of the flesh, the lust of the eyes and the pride of life* (I John 2:16). *It is enmity against God* (Romans 8:7). Whenever your emotions are heavily influencing a dream, the truth will appear to be clouded or ambiguous.

CHAPTER SIX:
THINGS WORTH MENTIONING

RUBBISH

Sometimes a dream has no meaning. There are some dreams that are just like the unwanted advertisements we receive in our mailbox, which we immediately throw in the trash. Try as you may, you will become frustrated before any meaning will emerge from a rubbish dream. Rubbish dreams can be the result of a racing mind, an over-active day or simply debris in the subconscious stream. Eccl. 5:7, *For in many dreams and in many words, there is emptiness. Rather fear God.*

They're nothing more than rubbish that should be discarded, giving them no credence for prophetic insight into your life. If you find yourself having more dreams that can't be salvaged rather than dreams of substance, you may need to debride your soul which is explained in the next chapter entitled, "Soul Cleansing Your Way to Dreaming".

Philippians 4:6-7 reminds us, *Don't be anxious but remember to pray and thank the Lord for hearing your request, then rest in Him knowing that the peace of God that passes all understanding will keep your heart and your mind healthy in Christ.*

YOUR CHILDHOOD AND YOUR DREAMS

Many have had the unfortunate experience of living through childhood abuse. Mental, physical and sexual abuse. I've spoken with men and women who were abused some or all of their adolescent and teen lives. Abuse leaves a stain on the soul. And in some cases, the stain becomes a wound that never healed. Many times, the spiritual wound would bleed, and the leaking blood could be seen by many.

Childhood abuse has a way of sabotaging al-most every area of a person's life. It adds toxemia to a marriage. Oftentimes, it's the root cause of rebellion to authority. Uncontrollable rage and anger, in many cases, is the by-product of abuse. The soul must be cleansed and healed from the ravages of abuse. Sexual perversion, unforgiveness and emotional trauma can greatly affect one's dreams. Cleansing these soul violations takes prayer, discipline, sometimes deliverance, and most of all forgiveness.

The abused must forgive the abuser. Unforgiveness is an enemy of the spirit, soul and body. If you do not forgive, you will never be able to reach your full potential in life. You will only ascend so high before you will meet up with the spirit of unforgiveness in your life and be forced to eradicate it.

I grew up in a home with a stepfather who was an abuser. I was the oldest of four girls, and the only one with a different father. My birth father died when I was two months old, so my stepfather was the only father figure I ever knew. He sexually abused everyone in the home as we were growing up. It made life a living hell.

As I became an adult, I held unforgiveness in

my heart towards him, particularly on behalf of my younger sisters. I even saw his death in a dream and exactly how he was going to die. It was a very painful death, and he died exactly as the Lord had revealed.

Many years later, God started dealing with me about my heart concerning him. I would always have disparaging things to say about him and started referring to him by his first name instead of as "Daddy" in conversations.

One morning as I was praying about my heart and unforgiveness, the Lord brought my stepfather before me. He showed me who He had made my stepfather to really be and how my stepfather was so broken by who he had become. In a vision I saw him crying because of his sins, and for the first time in my life, I understood what had not been clear to me all of my life. This man really didn't want to be the man he had become, and God showed me his repentant heart. All of my childhood and teenage years growing up, he never revealed that side of himself. I only saw him as cold and agnostic. At that moment, for the first time, I truly forgave him. Unforgiveness contaminates your soul. We must forgive.

CHAPTER SEVEN: SOUL CLEANSING YOUR WAY TO DREAMING

What is soul cleansing, and how do you know if you need it? If you have a history of reading your horoscope, consulting psychics, or have ever been to a spiritualist, there is a strong possibility you have ignorantly opened an entry of divination into your life. If this is the case, then severing that connection and commanding destruction upon its works is necessary. You are cleansing your soul of every connection that could facilitate an opening of divination manipulated and directed by the adversary.

Leviticus 19:31, *Do not turn to mediums or necromancers; do not seek them out, and so make yourselves unclean by them: I am the Lord your God.*

When reading that passage, the message is clear:

God does not approve of following a daily horoscope, relying on it for counsel. He doesn't approve of soliciting a psychic for answers or seeking counsel from those with familiar spirits. Practicing those habits will consequently wreak havoc for you.

If your bloodline includes practicing witches and warlocks who declared themselves as Clairvoyants or Spiritualists, that blood could be a portal for demonic transmission to generational successors. Those of you who frequently experience dreams that often place you in a room, a place, or a region where you are observing the activity rather than participating could possibly be experiencing signals of contamination. Work needs to be done to verify if the dream is good or bad, meaning from God or contaminated.

The following are examples of possible dream contamination:

- **Multiple scenes in dreams that have zero connection or line of reasoning**
- **Repeated dreams with deviant sexual acts**

- **Extreme abstract dreams**
- **Repeated nightmares**
- **Constant dreams of projection and flying, convoluted themes, and convoluted symbols**

The following are some questions to answer in order to determine if you have an outside influence in your dream state:

1. What spiritual giftings are in your bloodline?
2. Do you have anyone in your immediate or extended family who practice or practiced any form of the occult?
3. Was there and is there any type of abuse in your family? Physical or mental?
4. Do you have violent or vivid dreams?
5. Do you dream in color more than grayscale?
6. Do you have nightmares? If so, how often in a year?
7. While dreaming, has your body traveled to different places? If so, were you led out, or did

you travel on your own?

8. Do you frequently have out of body experiences while dreaming?

If you answered yes to questions 2-8 there has possibly been demonic infiltration into your dream state which needs to be eradicated immediately. There may be a need to go through deliverance prayer with a trusted Minister of the Gospel.

Portals can be opened through what may appear to be harmless holistic health practices such as Yoga, Reflexology, and Acupuncture. The human body does not have a built-in system that allows needles to be pushed through the skin and break it minus pain. How is that possible when the nerves directly under the surface of the skin are designed to sense pain, heat and noxious sensation? The average square inch of skin holds 650 sweat glands, 20 blood vessels and more than 1000 nerve endings. It is virtually impossible to push a needle through the skin and not feel pain "unless" the spirit world has been summoned to assist. The study of Taoism will shed more light on this subject.

If you have experienced childhood trauma in the form of sexual abuse, mental abuse, or physical abuse, professional counseling and therapy is always the best place to start the healing process. Revisiting the memories of your past and pushing the reset button through prayer and forgiveness will help to establish a release for you as well. We must forgive those whom have hurt us. We must set ourselves free by way of forgiveness. Ephesians 4:32 reminds us, *And be ye kind one to another, tenderhearted, forgiving one another, even as God for Christ's sake hath forgiven you.* Psalms 103:2-4, *Bless the Lord, O my soul, and forget not all his benefits: Who forgiveth all thine iniquities; who healeth all thy diseases; Who redeemeth thy life from destruction;*

God has redeemed us from the destruction of our past. Set today as the first day of the best days of your life and commit to walking in freedom from your past. See yourself being free from every weight that would attempt to hold you down. Your soul has to be free to dream unhindered. Free to hear the word of the Lord. Free to hear instructions tailor-made for you and you alone.

Being free from the weight of your past reminds me of the spiritual analogy of a marathon runner. Marathon trainers will express how important training is and how you must approach the 26 miles as a "marathon" and not a "sprint". What you eat, how long you prepare, and what you wear can make or break the run.

Eating inflammatory foods or wearing something as light as a cell phone can make the difference between winning or losing. The Word of God says in Hebrews 12:1 ...*getting rid of every weight that so easily besets us.* This command is very important when relating it to the health of our dream state.

As previously stated, it's never bad advice to seek out a therapist, a licensed professional who can treat and introduce healing from mental trauma. Stigmas of mental illness are often attached to those who seek help from a psychologist or a therapist, especially amongst those in our under-served communities. But mental therapy is one of the best self-care practices we can introduce into our lives. A word of caution: Beware of teachings of religious movements promising mental health. Demonic activity is attached to many of these practices, including spiritualists, spiritual energy, burning sage, esotericism, universalism and many more.

I LEAVE YOU WITH THIS

God's primary purpose is to make sons and daughters. Every dream He gives you will be geared towards ushering you into your life's purpose, building and guiding you into the spheres of influence you are called to have dominion in. If you do not know what your life's purpose is, you must be determined to find out. Your life will take on new meaning once you know why you were born. It is imperative that you are living in the purpose God created you for. The Word says, Your gift will make room for you and bring you before great men. (Proverbs 18:16) That has nothing to do with logistics in a building, but rather positioning. Your gift will make money for you because great men will be willing to treasure what God has placed inside of you. Do not neglect the gift that is within you, that was given to you through prophecy. (I Timothy 4:14) Again, it is imperative that you know why you were born. You must know your purpose. Your purpose is in lockstep with your gift. If you know you have a gift to interpret dreams, I encourage you to develop it. The Kingdom needs it. Dream interpretation is a mantle used to deliver God's people from imminent danger or destruction. It can propel one to victory. Dream interpretation is always an unveiling. It provides essential information that God downloads to the dreamer. DREAM ON!!

CHAPTER EIGHT: GLOSSARY[1]

ANIMALS

Alligator – Generational curse, ancient, evil spirit

Ant – Stinging or angry words, nuisance, industrious

Bat – Witchcraft: *And these are they which ye shall have in abomination among the fowls; they shall not be eaten, they are an abomination the bat. (Lev 11:13a,19b)*

Bear – Destroyer, destruction, an evil curse (through inheritance or personal sin, including financial loss or hardship)

Bees – Busybody, gossip, affliction

Bird – Holy Spirit, humanity

Black Bird – Demon spirit, gossip, slander, bitter words

Butterfly – Freedom, fragile

Cat – Self-willed, not trainable, stealthy, unclean spirit, deception, witchcraft: *With her much*

1. Permission from Author Ira Milligan-Destiny Images Copyright 2012/ISBN 13 TP:978-0-7684-4107-9

> *fair speech she caused him to yield, with the flattering of her lips (purring) she forced him (Proverbs 7:12,21)*

Chicken – Fear, cowardliness

Crow – Confusion, demonic spirit, spirit of envy or strife

Deer – Sure footed, graceful, swift

Dog – Strife, demonic spirit, offense

Donkey – Obnoxious, self-willed, unyielding

Dove – Holy Spirit, peace

Dragon – Spiritual warfare, the nation of China

Eagle – Prophet, leader, fierce predator, sorcerer

Elephant – Invincible, thick skinned, powerful

Fish – Soul of man, Holy Spirit

Fly – Demon, curse, unclean

Fox – Deception, cunning, wicked leader, false prophet

Frog – Witchcraft, demon, evil words

Goat – Sinner, negative person

Hornet – Affliction, biting words, slander

Horse – Time, work

Dead Horse – Lost cause

Kittens – Gift, precious, helpless

Lice – Shame, guilt, affliction

Lion – Dominion, Christ, satan, destroying spirit

Mice – Devourer, curse, plague

Monkey – Foolishness, clinging

Moth – Secret or undetectable trouble, deterioration

Owl – Wisdom, demon

Pig – Unbeliever, fornicator, unclean

Python – Divination, control, legalism

Rabbit – Fast growth

Raccoon – Mischief, deceitful, thief

Rat – Unclean, wicked person

Scorpion – Deception, destruction

Skunk – Offensive, something that should be put out

Snake – Demon, deception, threat, danger

Spider – Evil, sin, deception, temptation

Swine – Unclean, selfish, fornicator

Termite – Corruption, hidden destruction

Tiger – Immediate danger, powerful minister

Turkey – Foolish, clumsy

Vulture – Evil person, unclean

Wolf – Predator, devourer, false prophet, false minister

Worm – Corruption, evil

BUILDINGS, ROOMS, PLACES

Airport – Waiting, preparing, church, change

Attic – Mind, spiritual realm

Balcony – To oversee, spiritual insight

Bank – Church, dependable safe

Barbershop – Church, removal of old covenant

Basement – Carnal nature, hidden, secret

Bathroom – Cleansing, purging, strong lust

Beauty Shop – Church, preparation

Bedroom – Rest, intimacy, secret, good or evil covenant

Cafeteria – Helps, service, church work

Church Building – Possibly one's own church, congregation

Courthouse – Judgement, trial, persecution

Factory – Work or source, getting things done

Foundation – Established, stable, church government

Hospital – Church, place of healing

Hotel – Rest, temporary stop, church

House – Person, family, identity

New House – New life, change, new move

Old House – Past, inheritance, grandparent's ways

House Trailer – Temporary place, situation or relationship

Kitchen – Heart, intent, motive, plans

Library – Knowledge, education

Living Room – Current affairs, revealed, truth exposed

Mall – World

Motel – Same as Hotel

Office – Position of authority

Park – Rest, peace, vagrancy

Porch – Exposed, revealed

Prison – Bondage, rebellion

Restaurant – See Cafeteria

Roof – Covering, mind

School – Church, ministry, training

Tavern – Worldliness, escape from reality

Train Station – See airport

Zoo – Chaos, noisy strife, strange

COLORS

Black – Lack, grief, mourning, evil

Blue – Spiritual, divine revelation, spiritual gift

Light Blue – Spirit of man, evil spirit

Brown/Tan – Deadness, without spirit

Grey – Unclear, vague, grief

Green – Life, carnal, immature, inexperienced

Orange – Energy, great jeopardy, harm, danger

Pink – Flesh, sensual, immoral

Purple – Reign, noble

Red – Passion, emotion, anger

White – without mixture, unblemished

Yellow – Gift, fear, cowardly

DIRECTIONS

Back – Past, hidden, memory

Down – Worldly, humbled, demotion

Front – Now, future,

Left – Weakness, rejection

Right – Authority, power

Up – Advancement, promotion

NUMBERS

One – Beginning, new

Two – Divide, judge, separate

Three – Conform, imitate

Four – Reign, dominion

Five – Service, works, bondage

Six – Flesh, carnal

Seven – Finished, rest

Eight – Put off, new beginning

Nine – Harvest, fruitfulness

Ten – Measure, trial, test

Eleven – End, finished

Twelve – Government, joined, united

Thirteen – Rebellion, rejection, change

Fourteen – Double, reproduced

Fifteen – Grace, free, honor

Sixteen – Free spirited, without limitations

Seventeen – Incomplete, undeveloped, immature

Eighteen – Judgement, overcome, captivity

Nineteen – Barren, ashamed

Twenty – Holy, tried and approved

Hundred – Fullness, full recompense

Thousand – Maturity, full stature, mature judgment

PEOPLE

Actor – Role playing, insincere

Attorney – Advocate, Christ, accuser

Baby – New beginning, new project, new idea, new business

Bride – Church covenant

Brother – Self, natural brother, someone he reminds you of

Brother-in-law – Partiality or adversary, problem relationship

Carpenter – Builder, preacher

Dentist – Physician, fearful encounter

Doctor – Healer, Christ, preacher

Driver – Self, pastor, Christ, teacher

Drunk – Influenced, controlled, rebellious, self-indulging

Employer – Pastor, Christ, someone he or she resembles

Family – Spiritual family

Father – Christ, authority

Friend – Self, someone's friend represents another – look for similar initials

Grandchild – Heir, oneself, spiritual legacy

Grandmother/Grandfather – Spiritual inheritance

Husband – Authority, Christ, a divorcee's first husband sometimes represents the world

Judge – Authority, conscience

Man – Stranger, angel, oneself, demon

Mother – Source: church, spiritual mother

Mother-in-law – legalistic church, meddler, trouble

One's Children – Oneself or themselves, church members

Police – Authority, enforcer, angel

Preacher – Messenger, spiritual authority good or evil

Sister – Self, someone she reminds you of

Thief – Deceiver, unexpected loss, satan, fraud

Wife – Covenant, joined, church

Witch – control, evil influence, seduction

Woman – Stranger, seducing spirit, temptation

VEHICLES

Airplane – Person, work, church

Jet – Ministry or minister

Ambulance – Urgent need, salvation, emergency

Automobile – Person, ministry – New Car = new ministry, new project

Convertible – Uncovered in a situation, attitude

Auto Accident – Strife, conflict, confrontation

Bicycle – Works of the flesh

Boat – Support, person, recreation

Bus – Ministry,

School Bus – Teaching

Helicopter – Individual, the church

Motorcycle – Personal ministry, selfish, pride

Moving Van – Change

Pickup Truck – Work, personal ministry,
natural work

Rearview Mirror – Driving backwards, looking back

Roller Coaster – Unstable, trials, excitement

Tires – Spirit, life, spiritual condition

Train – Continuous, unceasing work

SUV – Family, church family

CPSIA information can be obtained
at www.ICGtesting.com
Printed in the USA
BVHW081043240221
600895BV00003B/604

9 781513 664125